Family Life Illustrated

For PARENTS

RONNIE FLOYD

Family Life Illustrated

For PARENTS

RONNIE FLOYD

New Leaf Press

Family Life Illustrated for Parents

First printing: November 2004

ISBN: 0-89221-588-7
Library of Congress Number: 2004106960

Cover concept by Left Coast Design, Portland, OR

All sidebar statistics have been provided by: The Barna Group Online, 1957 Eastman Ave Ste B, Ventura, CA 93003. (www.barna.org/FlexPage.aspx?Page=Topic&TopicID=20)

Printed in the United States of America

Please visit our website for other great titles:
www.newleafpress.net

For information regarding author interviews,
please contact the publicity department
at (870) 438-5288.

CONTENTS

Great Parents Rule!

NOTHING you do in your life will be as important as how you raise your children.

"Success" comes in all sizes and shapes and colors, but success can be deceptive. Materialism and selfishness can masquerade as success, but, please hear me: Daddy and Mother must raise their children in Christian love. Any other standard is doomed to fail.

Jeana and I raised our boys to walk with God. Their other "successes" in life are satisfying, but our sons will spend eternity with us and that trumps all. Sometimes when I walk the sidelines on a cool fall evening, shouting at my son's high school football team to drive for another score, I watch him and marvel. His very life was entrusted to me by our Creator, and I'm

Where will your children spend eternity? Chances are, if you're reading this book, you are a Christian. You've thought about these things. But even if you are an atheist — be honest — you've wondered about what happens beyond this life. Perhaps you give your children everything. Maybe they are on top of the world.

But are you raising them to do what Solomon said is the chief aim of humans: to fear God and follow his laws?

here to tell you: I purposed in my heart not to fail.

Where are you with your children? Are you satisfied, content, at peace? I could ask you a lot of things about their lives. Do they make good grades? Are they drug-free? Nurtured?

All those are well and good, but let's take it to another level, the ultimate level.

Where will your children spend eternity?

Chapter 1

A Tough but Rewarding Job

IF you don't want to learn new things, don't ever have children. Children have a way of teaching us more than we probably want to know. Consider just a few things that children have taught me at our church.

First, I've learned that during prayer — with every adult eye closed — anything can happen in a room of full of preschoolers. I have also learned that a fire extinguisher is a very handy device. I have learned that Kool-Aid and songs with hand motions do not mix. I have learned that animal crackers can be sneezed out the nose, and that vomit comes in all colors.

Children teach us a lot of things. And one of the

biggest things they teach us is that parenting is one tough job.

The other day I came across a parent's job description. See if you qualify:

Long-term player needed for challenging, permanent work in a chaotic environment. Candidates must possess excellent communication and organizational skills and be willing to work evenings and weekends and frequent 24-hour shifts. Some overnight travel is required, including trips to primitive camping sites on rainy weekends and endless sports tournaments in faraway cities. Travel expenses are not reimbursed.

You must keep this job for the rest of your life and be willing to be hated, at least temporarily. You must be willing to bite your tongue repeatedly and possess the physical stamina of a pack mule. You must be willing to tackle stimulating technical challenges, as of gadget repair, sluggish toilets, and stuck zippers. You must handle assembling and product safety testing, as well as floor maintenance and janitorial work.

> *Parenting is not easy work. . . . It takes concentration and focus.*

You must screen phone calls, maintain calendars, and coordinate production of multiple homework projects. You must have the ability to plan and organize social gatherings for clients of all ages and levels of maturity. You must be willing to be indispensable one minute and an embarrassment the next. You must assume final and complete accountability for the quality of the end product.

There is no possibility for advancement. Your job is to remain in the same position for years without complaining, so those in your charge can ultimately surpass you. No previous experience required, but on-the-job training is offered on a continually exhausting basis.

Although you will receive no financial compensation, you must pay those in your charge, offering frequent wages and bonuses. A balloon payment is due when they turn 18 and attend college. And when you die, you give them whatever income you have left.

Parenting is not easy work. It's hard and it's tough. It takes concentration and focus. Often you learn only through failure. Many days you wonder why God gave children to young men and women with no clue what they're doing. And often you find yourself agreeing wholeheartedly with the disgruntled man who said, "Children today are tyrants. They contradict their parents, they gobble their food, they terrorize their teachers."

Are you nodding your head? Do you tend to think that children today are worse than they have ever been?

If so, then consider that the statement quoted above came from the ancient Greek philosopher Socrates, *way back in 426 B.C.!*

Parenting has always been an enormous challenge. Out of all things in life in which I've had the privilege to participate — whether a ministry, a job, sports, recreation, or anything else — I have found *nothing* more challenging than parenting. Nothing can bring you more grief than parenting.

But at the same time, nothing will bring you greater joy than parenting.

Nothing will feel more rewarding.

With so much at stake, a lot of us feel confused about how to raise our kids. So many radically different opinions and techniques and philosophies on child rearing exist today. It makes you wonder, *What is the right way to raise a kid?*

Is there one best way? And if so, what is it? Which way should we go?

Teach Us What to Do

I'd like to introduce you to a man named Manoah. Manoah and his wife lived long ago in the days of the Judges in ancient Israel. The couple tried to have a family, but for a long time remained childless.

Then one day an angel of God appeared to this anxious husband and wife and told them that they were going to have a baby boy. The couple greeted the news with great delight, but also with some apprehension. Soon after the angel had left them, Manoah cried out to God, "Oh LORD, please let the man of God whom you have sent come to us again that he may teach us what to do for the boy who is to be born" (Judg. 13:8).

Teach us what to do for the boy who is to be born.

. . . nothing will bring you greater joy than parenting.

This wise couple knew that although they desperately wanted a child, they did not know how to raise him properly. So they asked the Lord for help and instruction and guidance — and God gave it to them.

Eventually Manoah and his wife had a son by the name of Samson. The boy grew up to become a Bible-sized hero destined to help deliver his people from the brutal power of their oppressors. The Spirit of God came upon Samson at a young age and the blessing of God rested on his life.

What would have happened, do you think, if Samson's parents had not cried out, "Teach us what to do for the boy"? I don't know, but neither do I want to know. A prayer like this ought to be on the

> *Our children should be able to imitate what we do, and what they imitate should bring great glory to God.*

lips of every one of us as parents. "Dear God, teach us what to do for our children! Teach me what to do for my girl! Teach me what to do for my boy!"

Call it Parenting 101.

When we make this our prayer, we quickly make a crucial discovery. We learn that we have one major and overriding responsibility as parents: to model Jesus Christ and His ways to our children so that they will want to follow Him for themselves. That is our single biggest duty as godly parents, to model Jesus Christ and His ways to our children so that they will want to follow Him for themselves.

And what is a model?

A model is a standard, an example for imitation.

As parents, we should set the standard for our children and provide an example for them. Our children should be able to imitate what we do, and what they imitate should bring great glory to God. God wants us to create children in our mold, because we're in the mold of Jesus Christ, the Son of God, our Living Savior.

In this little book I want to capitalize on that word "model." I want to mine the Word of God for some of its wisdom on parenting, and present to you what I've found in the form of an acrostic. What follows are some life skills for parenting, part of the divine curricula for Parenting 101:

M Move your children to God at a young age

O Open your heart to your children

D Discipline your children

E Eliminate unnecessary stuff

L Love your children unconditionally

Without question, parenting is a tough but rewarding job. You really can do it, though — so long as you follow the example of Manoah and with a sincere heart cry out to God, "Teach me what to do for this child!"

And now is as good a time as any to get down on your knees.

Chapter 2

Move Your Children to God

WHEN you get on an airplane, what do you intend to do? Do you want to fly, oh, just anywhere the pilot wants to go? Hardly. Most likely, you have a definite destination in mind. If you want to go to New York, you don't want to touch down in Tuba City, Arizona. You want to reach a specified destination.

Unfortunately, far too many of us fail to give our children a proper destination for *life*. This is why so many of us consistently interact with our kids on a negative footing. "Don't do this, don't do that," we say. "No, no, no, no, no, *no!*"

May I ask a question? What are you giving your children to say *yes* to?

Parenting is not all about the no's. It's not about all of the things to avoid. It is much more about what your children can say yes to in life.

One of the greatest things a parent can do for a child is to help define a vision for that son or daughter's life — to set a destination, in other words. Many bewildered children reach young adulthood with no clue about what to do with their life because their parents never helped them define a vision for their life. Mom and Dad never helped them set a life destination.

What about you? Are you assisting your child in setting a life destination? Are you helping your child to develop a vision for his or her young life?

According to the Bible, by far the most important life lesson you can ever deposit in your children is to teach them to unreservedly, unapologetically, and unashamedly love the Lord their God with all of their might.

Love for God Above All Else

Deuteronomy 6:5 declares, "You shall love the LORD your God with all your heart, with all your soul, and with all your strength." Jesus identified this as the most important commandment in Scripture (Mark 12:29–30). *This* is what the Christian life is all about!

> . . . *first, we are to love the Lord with all of our "heart."*

This verse tells us that, first, we are to love the Lord with all of our "heart." Our heart represents our deepest *emotions*. God calls us to love Him with genuine and strong emotion — and that means our love for Him can't be a mere intellectual nod or a casual mental acceptance of His rightful place in our life. It has to be real. It has to be vibrant.

Second, we are to love God with all of our "soul." Our soul includes the mind and the will. Jesus made this explicit when He said, "Love the Lord your God with all your heart and with all your soul *and with all your mind*" (Mark 12:30, emphasis added). Our love for God is to be thoughtful, reflective, and carefully considered. It is to be intelligent.

Third, we are to love God with all of our strength. The word translated "strength" is the Hebrew term for "might." This love of ours for God is never lazy, but taps into every bit of power that our bodies can muster. It is a muscular love.

Put it all together, and we are to love God with all that we have and with all that we are. God wants us to express total adoration for Him. He wants us to feel and act passionately toward Him. He calls every one of us to passionately love the Lord our God, without any reservations, with wholehearted commitment, eagerly expressing our love to God alone.

May I ask — do *you* love the Lord with no reservations? Do *you* love Him with wholehearted commitment? Do *you* express your deepest love to Him alone?

Because this is serious stuff that goes to the core of who we are, the very next verse says, "And these words which I command you today shall be in your heart." This command to love God passionately, with full and complete commitment, is to take root "in your heart," in the deepest and truest part of your being.

Now, keep in mind that these statements are all given to *parents*. That means that if your kids are going to "get it," you must first "get it" in your own

Checking the facts

57%

39%

Closer to Mother

Closer to Father

Teens appear to be closer to their mothers than their fathers, with 57% of U.S. teens indicating that they are emotionally close with their mothers compared to 39% of teens indicating that they are emotionally close to their fathers.

(1999) www.barna.org

heart. If you are going to teach your children to love God with their whole hearts, then you must first love God with your whole heart.

Our children grow up to be unapologetic about their faith only when they see Mom and Dad standing courageously in their own faith. And that takes passion.

If your little girl asked for your help on becoming a cheerleader or getting in the band or preparing to be class president, how would you react if she received your counsel and help with a yawn and a nap? Or if you were teaching your son how to play football or soccer or how to fix a car, and he had a lazy attitude about it, what would you do? You'd probably immediately get on him and say, "Man, if you want to get better at this, you have to make a commitment to it!"

Many of us are raising kids committed to everything in the world except the only thing that ultimately matters. God didn't tell us to spend all of our time teaching our children how to pursue things that in eternity will count for nothing. But God does tell us that if we will just teach our kids how to love the Lord their God with all of their heart, soul, and might, then all the rest will fall into proper order.

What are you passionate about today? Be certain of this: your kids will "get it,"

> *What are you passionate about today?*

whatever it is. Your son or daughter will "get" what makes you passionate.

Teach Them Diligently, Continually, Everywhere

The Bible doesn't leave us in the dark about how to teach our children to love God with all of their heart, soul, and might. It tells us, "You shall teach [these words about loving God] diligently to your children and shall talk of them when you sit in your house, when you walk by the way, when you lie down, and when you rise up" (Deut. 6:7).

How are we to teach our children to love the Lord with all their heart, with all of their soul, and with all of their strength? We are to do so "diligently," which means consistently and continually.

Whenever you talk to your kids, talk to them about loving the Lord.

> *Whenever you talk to your kids, talk to them about loving the Lord.*

When you sit together in your home, talk to them about loving the Lord.

When you walk to the store, talk to them about loving the Lord. When you put them to bed at night, talk to them about loving the Lord. When you get up the next morning, talk to them about loving the Lord.

Parenting, in other words, is a full-time job. That means we cannot get it done in one minute. There is no such thing as a "one-minute" parent. Parenting cannot be done as we rush through the house on our way to work. Parenting is a full-time job.

It's also a very personal job. Verse 8 says, "You shall bind them [these words about loving God] as a sign on your hand and they shall be as frontlets between your eyes." Give yourself signals throughout the day to remind you to love the Lord your God with all of your heart, soul, and mind. In ancient Israel they took actual portions of Scripture and placed them in little boxes, then used straps of leather to tie those boxes around their fore-head and upon their hands, to remind them all during the day to love the Lord their God with all of their heart, soul, and strength.

And then they took it a step further. Verse 9 says, "You shall write them [these words about loving God] on the doorpost of your house and on your gates." Orthodox Jews wrote this passage upon their doorpost as a blessing to their home, to remind everyone inside that they were to love their God with all of their heart, with all of their soul, and with all of their strength.

Do we still need such reminders today? Absolutely! And so do our children.

When my boys used to leave the house to spend the night with a friend or to go somewhere else, I made it a habit to speak one special phrase to them before they left: "Remember to whom you belong." I didn't tell them to remember who they were; I urged them to remember to whom they belonged. They belonged (and still do) to Christ.

As a parent, you are to model for your children how to love the Lord your God with all your heart, soul and strength, from the moment you get up in the morning until the moment you lay your head on the pillow at night. This is your number-one calling as a parent.

A Few Practical Suggestions

While I could suggest several practical ways to help you fulfill your number one parental calling, let me focus on just four. In my opinion, these four will do you more good than a hundred others.

1. Pray with your children daily.

Do you pray with your children? Do you mentor your children in prayer?

I remember times in our home from years past when my little guys would start rambling off some prayer — and I would stop them. "Now, did you mean that?"

I'd ask. And I'd call them to account-ability. "Don't just run through vain repetitions," I would say, "mean it in your heart. Make it count for the cause of Christ."

> *If you never pray with . . . your children, why should your children ever have a strong conviction about the importance of prayer?*

If you never pray with and over your children, why should your children ever have a strong conviction about the importance of prayer? Every morning I tried to pray over my boys before they went off to school, and if I couldn't do it, Jeana did. It didn't have to be some long dialogue. Sometimes it might be 20 seconds; sometimes a minute; sometimes 2 or 3 minutes. When you send off your children with prayer, they understand at least one thing: *our family believes in prayer*. And as much as they may appreciate it today, they're going to appreciate it a lot more 20 years from now.

2. At a very young age, teach them how to have a quiet time.

Your kids ought to grow up in a home where they see their parents have a daily quiet time with God. Do you know why so many of us, even as adults, have inconsistent times with God? Usually it's because nobody taught us as young people the importance of having a vital quiet time with the Lord.

But understand this: time spent with God is essential to loving God. Imagine trying to tell your spouse or fiancé, "I love you, but I don't want to spend any time with you." Who's going to buy that? Unless we teach our kids how to spend time alone with God, they're going to have an awfully rough time learning how to love Him when they get older.

From the very beginning, my wife and I taught our sons, Josh and Nick, the importance of hav-ing a time alone with God. If I'm not mistaken, Josh read the whole Bible through in a year, even as a little guy. I taught both my boys how to read the Word. I taught them how to write prayers to God. I taught them how to journal.

Check in on your kids once a week or so, giving them something simple to read. I probably gave mine too much, too soon, but so far it hasn't appeared to hurt either one of them. I have yet to see anyone overdose on the Word of God!

Sunday is not to be a day of fishing and golfing and shopping and soccer and baseball and football and basketball and camping and family reunions.

3. Teach them the value of worship on the Lord's Day.

Sunday is a holy day before God. It is to be a day of celebrating the resurrection of Christ, a day of reflection on the past week and anticipation of the week to come.

God created us to worship. On the first day of the week we are to gather as a congregation and give praise to the Lord Jesus Christ. And realize that you cannot teach your children the value of the worship on the Lord's Day if you don't observe it in your own life. Sunday is not to be a day of fishing and golfing and shopping and soccer and baseball and football and basketball and camping and family reunions. Sunday is the Lord's Day. And the number-one agenda item on the Lord's Day is to worship God with His people. My parents raised me this way, and it "took." My mother and dad would never have thought of doing anything else on the Lord's Day.

Bring your children to church. Get them involved in the preschool ministry, in the children's ministry, in the youth ministry, in the student ministry, in the college ministry. And let the church help you to teach your kids how to love God with passion.

4. Help them sort out their friends.

Show me a Christian kid struggling with his faith, and I'll show you a kid who has collected one or more friends who have led him away from God.

Make sure that your kids collect friends who reflect the values you try to teach them!

Do everything you can to influence — and sometimes, even control — your kids' choice of friends. Ungodly friends will lead your children away from the heart of God quicker than anything else in the world. "Do not be misled," Paul writes. "Bad company corrupts good character" (1 Cor. 15:33). On the other hand, friends who genuinely love God can help your children through the roughest of spots, as a discouraged David once found out: "And Saul's son Jonathan went to David at Horesh and helped him find strength in God" (1 Sam. 23:16).

Don't Wait

I don't mean to pry, but — have you taught your children how to walk with God?

"Oh, I'm going to wait till they're teenagers."

Listen, if you wait that long, it'll be too late. The frontlines are no longer in the 7th grade; the frontlines have moved to elementary school. The battlefield has

Do everything you can to influence . . . your kids' choice of friends.

already come to the littlest kids. Satan wants to take those innocent children captive — and one of the best ways to defeat him is to lead your small child to Christ, and then teach him or her how to walk with God.

Parents, move your children close to God at a young age! Win your kids to Christ as early as possible! Don't wait until they are all grown up, hoping they will "get it" later on. The longer they wait to follow Christ, the less likely the chance that they will ever come to the Lord. While they're still young, win them to a saving relationship with Jesus Christ. And then teach them how to walk with Him. This is an extremely hard lesson to give, by the way, if we don't practice it ourselves.

So model a passionate walk with Jesus Christ! Model a passionate love for the church! When you do, your kids stand a much greater chance of walking in the ways of the Lord. And then they can experience for themselves the kind of blessing enjoyed by Uzziah, a godly king of ancient Israel:

> As long as he sought the LORD, God gave him success (2 Chron. 26:5).

Teach your children to love the Lord with all their heart, soul, and might — and so set them up for success. No parent can do more.

Chapter 3

Open Your Heart

AS the firestorm known as World War II raged across the planet, one sad and regretful father took pen in hand to write a note of encouragement (and apology) to his grown son, then fighting on some distant, foreign battleground. Here is what he wrote:

Dear Son,
I wish I had the power to write
The thoughts
wedged in my
heart tonight
As I sit watching that
small star
And wondering
where and how
you are.
You know, Son, it's
a funny thing
How close a war can
really bring

A father who for
   years with pride
Has kept emotion
   deep inside.
I'm sorry, Son, when
   you were small
I let reserve build up
   that wall.
I told you, "Real
   men never cry."
And it was Mom
   who always dried
Your tears and

smoothed your
   hurts away
So that you soon
   went back to play.
But, Son, deep down
   within my heart
I longed to have
   some little part
In drying that small
   tear-stained face.
But we were men.
Men don't embrace.
Suddenly I found
   my son
A full grown man
   with childhood
   done.
Tonight you're far
   across the sea
Fighting away for
   men like me.
Well, somehow
   pride and what is
   right
Have somehow
   changed places

here tonight.
I find my eyes won't
    stay quite dry
And that real men
    sometimes do cry.
And if we stood here
    face to face,
I'm sure, my Son, we
    would embrace.[1]

How many parents have
looked back over the long
years and regretted the
terrible emotional distance

*You can open your heart
to your children.*

that they allowed to grow
between them and their
children? They wished that

they had reached out, cried
together, embraced. They
regret that they never fully
opened their hearts.

For such parents, what's
done is done. The years
have marched on. These
moms and dads might,
with great difficulty, be
able to repair some of the
damage — but those early
years of parenting, and the
opportunities they pre-
sented, have disappeared
forever, and no one
can do anything to
change what hap-
pened.

Thank God
that the story can
be very different
for you! You can put into
place a plan of action that
will keep you from having

to write such a mournful letter to your own child in years to come. You can make the choice to really connect with your kids, to cherish them, treasure them, and let them know how much they mean to you.

You can open your heart to your children.

A Free Flow of Affection

What does it mean to open your heart to your children? It means that you beckon them inside your life. It means that you treat them with such honor and tenderness that eventually they return the favor. It means that you treasure them as the gifts from God that they really are (see Ps. 127:3). It means that you look for ways to show your children how delighted you feel that God has put them in your life.

In a remarkable passage in the Book of Second Corinthians, the apostle Paul illustrates what it means to "open our hearts." Remember that the believers in this church had caused Paul no end of trouble. They sparred with one another, formed exclusive and snobbish cliques, neglected those who most needed attention, slandered Paul, and even endorsed the most repulsive kind of sexual immorality. You'd think that Paul would blast them, scorch them, read them the riot act, and tan their behinds. Yet listen to what he writes to these wayward young believers in Christ:

We have spoken freely to you, Corinthians, and opened wide our hearts to you. We are not withholding our affection from you, but you are withholding yours from us. As a fair exchange — I speak as to my children — open wide your hearts also (2 Cor. 6:11–13; NIV).

Paul considered the Corinthians his "children" — naughty children, to be sure. But he loved them nonetheless. He tells them he has "opened wide" his heart to them. He reassures them that he has not withheld his "affection" from them. And he lets them know how much he would like to feel the same depth of warmth from them toward him. He doesn't insist on it, of course — he was wise enough to know that affection can only be given, not taken — yet through both words and actions he reminds the Corinthians how much he cares for them, thinks of them, loves them.

I wonder, have you opened your heart to your children? Do they know, both by your actions and your words, that you delight in them? When they look at you, do they see a parent whose heart has opened wide to them?

A Listening Heart

Parents, open your heart to your children. One good way to do this is to make sure that you listen carefully to them and to their concerns — *really* listen.

"To be a good listener," writes one mother, "you must *want* to hear what your child has to say. You have to believe that your youngster's thoughts and feelings are important, and that he gains tremendous benefits from your listening."[2] She recommends that parents make listening a conscious commitment and cites a survey in which young people were asked what they wanted most from their parents. The overwhelming response?

> *. . . look for ways to show your children how delighted you feel that God has put them in your life.*

"They desired that their parents take time to listen to them and understand them."[3]

When you listen, make sure that you keep your eye on your child. Don't allow yourself to scan the room or gaze out the window. Loss of eye contact communicates the message, "What you're saying isn't really all that important, so while I'm going to pretend to listen, really I'm going to be thinking about something else that actually matters to me." When you listen, *really* listen.

Remember that God in His Word tells us, *"everyone*

> *Work hard to create a home environment in which your children can say anything to you about anything in life. . . .*

should be quick to listen, slow to speak . . ." (James 1:19; NIV). That "everyone" includes us, parents. And when we work at being quick to listen to our kids, they'll see in us a heart wide open to them and their concerns.

A Communicating Heart

Parents, open your heart to your children. Let them know what's on your mind and what you believe about the important issues of life. Encourage conversation, even when it feels tough. Let them know that you're always open for business when it comes to honest discussion. Talk to them not only about the Lord, but about everything. Don't be afraid to talk about anything.

Talk to them about being kids.
Talk to them about school.
Talk to them about friends.
Talk to them about money.

Talk to them about drugs.

Talk to them about sex.

Talk to them about parenting.

Talk to them about life.

Talk to them about *everything*.

Work hard to create a home environment in which your children can say anything to you about anything in life, without fear that you will immediately judge them. When you do this, you will find that, in time — when they determine it's right — they will open their heart to you. And then they will eagerly reciprocate what you have done for them.

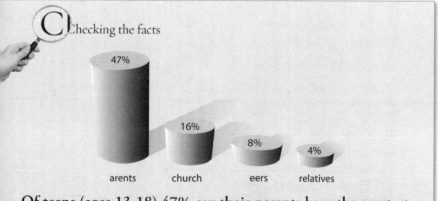

Checking the facts

47%

16%

8%

4%

arents   church   eers   relatives

Of teens (ages 13-18) 47% say their parents have the greatest influence on their spiritual development; 16% listed their church; 8% named peers; 4% said relatives. (1998) www.barna.org

I know, of course, that this isn't easy. Our kids can clam up tighter than an oyster under attack by a hungry starfish. Proverbs 20:5 tells us, "The purposes of a man's heart are deep waters, but a man of understanding draws them out." The purposes of a teenager's heart are also deep waters (often turbulent!), and if you want to draw them out, you need to be a parent of understanding . . . and patience. Understand that if you really want your child to open up, you must first clearly demonstrate that you have an open heart.

A Participating Heart

To have an open heart toward your children also requires that you participate with them in their world. It doesn't matter whether this means attending ball games, watching gymnastics together, following special interests, flying paper airplanes, or whatever else it might be. To have an open heart is to participate with your child in his or her world.

A heartbreaking story headlined "A Lesson for Fathers" illustrates this truth for me. Ron Lee Davis wrote the following in a small town newspaper column:

There was a little boy who kept asking his father, "Dad, will you come out to the back yard and help me build a treehouse?" And this boy's father, always with the best intentions, said, "Sure, son — but later, okay? I'm really busy right now, but we'll build that treehouse real soon." Many times this boy asked his father that question; the answer was always the same.

But one day, this little boy got hit by a car. As he lay dying in the hospital, one of the last things he said to his dad was, "Well, Dad, I guess we'll never get to build that tree-house."

This is a true story. I officiated at that little boy's funeral.[4]

To have an open heart is to participate with your child in his or her world.

We cannot show our children that we love them if we're continually running around the country trying to figure out how to make more money, or how to become better at what we do, and therefore never participate with them in what *they* do.

Over the years I cancelled several speaking engagements because I wanted to be at my kids' activities. I wanted to show them that I loved them and was very interested in their world. I wanted them to see my heart wide open to them.

I like an old cartoon strip by Bruce Hammond. In one strip, the main character, a middle-aged businessman named Duffy, is sitting at a desk buried under piles of important papers. He's on the phone with his boss, who seems not at all happy with our hero.

"Duffy!" the man screams, "I thought you were going to put together a sales analysis over the weekend! Where is it?"

Duffy replies, "I, uh, didn't get around to it, W.G."

"Didn't get around to it?!" his boss explodes. "And why not?!?"

"Lessee," Duffy responds. "I shot a couple of rounds of golf with my son on Saturday, then treated myself to dinner out and a movie. On Sunday I did the crossword puzzle, and spent the rest of the day with my grandkids."

"Well, I think it's high time you re-examine your priorities!" yells W.G.

Duffy leans back in his chair, puts his

> *The parent must become a master at grabbing the teachable, everyday moment.*

foot up on his knee and says simply, "I did."[5]

Be Open to Life Lessons

To have an open heart also means to remain open to the proverbial "teachable moment," to that incident or circumstance that "just happens" in the course of everyday events, one that you can use to teach your children valuable lessons. I think these moments, rightly captured, can do our kids more good than a hundred more formal (and less welcomed) episodes. I agree with author Karen Mains when she writes:

> I believe the best spiritual growth comes when truth is applied to a child's everyday living, when the experiences and traumas and perplexities of common life are mixed with God's ideas, resulting in a nourishing fertilizer that enriches the soul.
>
> Spiritual truth disassociated from everyday experience creates a disadvantageous growing environment, an inadequate spiritual ecology. The parent must become a master at grabbing the teachable, everyday moment. He or she must develop the ability to create compost, to pile on the stuff of everyday existence, and to mix it with spiritual truth.[6]

"What's the recipe for a spiritual compost pile that will make your children grow?" Mains asks. "It's the stuff of daily ingredients mixed with a spiritually alert parent who is also growing spiritually, layered with Scripture that fits the experience, applied morning, noon, and night, all covered over with a carpet of prayer. When such a mixture is shoveled on the family faith garden, it will fertilize, mulch, enrich, and heat the innermost self until it fully ripens before God."[7]

I don't believe that you need to teach your kids a Bible study for an hour and a half every night. I doubt they'll respond to that very well, unless you are some kind of phenomenal Bible teacher and they're some kind of unique kids. But when various events happen, you *can* teach them what the Word of God says through on-the-spot life lessons.

You'll be able to do so, however, only if you consciously cultivate that open heart.

Only One Shot

Fellow parents, we get only one shot at parenting. There are no dress rehearsals. Although we're bound to make mistakes, that doesn't have to prevent us from giving it our best shot.

Open your heart to your child! It's hard to think of a better shot than that.

Endnotes

1. James S. Hewett, editor, *Illustrations Unlimited* (Wheaton, IL: Tyndale House Publishers, 1988), p. 200–201.

2. C. Joanne Sloan, "Listen To Your Children!" *Focus on the Family* magazine, October 1987, p. 10.

3. Ibid., p. 11.

4. Dr. Ron Lee Davis, "A Lesson for Fathers," source unknown.

5. Bruce Hammond, "Duffy," 1991, Universal Press Syndicate.

6. Karen Mains, *Living, Loving, Leading* (Portland, OR: Multnomah Press, n.d.), p. 156.

7. Ibid., p. 165.

We were visiting friends when they received a telephone call from their recently married daughter. After several tense minutes on the phone, the mother told the father to pick up the extension. The newlyweds had had their first big fight. In a few moments, the father rejoined us and tersely explained, "Said she wanted to come home." "What did you tell her?" I asked. "Told her she was home."

– Larry Cunningham (Billings, Montana),
Reader's Digest

Chapter 4

Discipline Your Kids

KIDS will try some very interesting things. Often, we parents don't know the things they try until after they've tried them. How would you respond to a son or daughter who said to you:

- No matter how hard you try, you can't baptize cats.

- If your sister hits you, don't hit her back; they always catch the second person.

- Never ask your three-old-brother to hold a tomato.

- You can't trust dogs to watch your food.

- Puppies still have bad breath, even after eating a Tic Tac.

- Never hold a dust buster and a cat at the same time.

- Some school lunches can stick to cafeteria walls.

If you ever hear your child say anything like this, probably you can expect that at least two tasks lie in your immediate future:

1. Some level of repair is required;

2. Some discipline is in order.

What Is Discipline?

The Bible has a lot to say about discipline. The Hebrew words most commonly translated "discipline" (*yasar* and *musar*) appear in the Old Testament almost 90 times. They point primarily to a God-centered way of life, and only secondarily to decent behavior. Most often, the terms refer to oral instruction rather than corporal punishment. In general, they speak of correction resulting in education leading to positive changes in behavior.[1]

In the New Testament, the Greek word for

"discipline" *(paidea)* usually refers to training, education, and discipline. It, too, describes correction that leads to reformation. Time and again, the Word of God instructs parents to discipline their children, sometimes (but not usually) by physical means. Consider just a few verses from the Book of Proverbs (NIV):

> Discipline your son, for in that there is hope; do not be a willing party to his death (Prov. 19:18).

If you love your children, you will discipline them.

Discipline your son, and he will give you peace; he will bring delight to your soul (Prov. 29:17).

> He who spares the rod hates his son, but he who loves him is careful to discipline him (Prov. 13:24).

> Folly is bound up in the heart of a child, but the rod of discipline will drive it far from him (Prov. 22:15).

> Do not withhold discipline from a child; if you punish him with the rod, he

will not die. Punish him with the rod and save his soul from death (Prov. 23:13–14).

If you love your children, you will discipline them. You will set clear boundaries for them. You will instruct them in the right way to go. You will help them to develop the kind of self-control that will enable them to succeed throughout life.

If you do not discipline them, however — if you do not exercise some control over them and restrain them from foolish behavior when they're young — then sooner or later they will end up in a life of sin, misery, and even lawlessness. If you will be serious about this, you'll reap the benefits. And so will your kids.

Teach Them about Biblical Authority

If we're going to teach our children how to love God, then we're going to have to discipline them. And to discipline them properly we need first to teach them about biblical authority.

It is crucial that our children understand the authority of the Bible. I have told my sons throughout their lives that the Bible is God's Holy Word, without any error in it, at all, anywhere. I have trained them to know that the authority in our home resides not in what I say or in what Jeana says, but in what God says in His Word. Our authority is God's Word.

The Word of God helps us to choose our friends. It guides us in what we are to do. It determines where we should go. It teaches us what we should watch and what we should say. That's why the Apostle Paul can write, "All Scripture is God-breathed and is useful for teaching, rebuking, correcting, and training in righteousness, so that the man of God may be thoroughly equipped for every good work" (2 Tim. 3:16–17; NIV).

If you want to be a successful Christian parent, then you *must* learn how to accept and live by the authority of the Word of God. Ask yourself, "Is the Bible my authority? Do I live by its wisdom and its instruction? Do I allow it to instruct me in every area of life?"

Every person in the world operates according to some authority. Every parent on the globe makes parenting choices by consulting some authority.

For some of us, that authority might be personal experience. But since such an approach amounts to little more than trial and error, it often leads to unnecessary pain and sometimes to disaster.

For others of us, that authority is our culture. It's the culture speaking when your second or third grader says, "Everybody else is doing it!" after you forbid him to do something he begs to do. A thousand times or more my boys have heard my standard reply to this objection. Eventually it became a joke in our home: "Well, if so and so jumps off a cliff, are you going to fall off the cliff with him?" After awhile, I didn't have to give "the speech" much anymore; my sons had begun to understand the authority of the Bible.

For still others, that authority is personal preference or opinion. But do you know what inevitably happens in such a home? Since your preferences and opinions differ markedly from your children's, a se-

ries of heated clashes erupt between you and them. And anger reigns.

We all need to be able to look at our children and

> *If you want to be a successful Christian parent, then you must learn how to accept and live by the authority of the Word of God.*

say, "Remember, the Bible is the final authority in our home, so this is what we're going to do." Teach your children that the Bible is the Word of God. Teach them that it is the final authority in your home. And then discipline them according to its wisdom.

Discipline With Love

When many people think of discipline, words like "harsh" and "punishment" and "painful" tend to come to mind. But biblical discipline is always done in love, for the benefit of the one being disciplined. Remember Proverbs 19:18? It says, "Discipline your son while there is hope and do not desire his death." In other words, if you don't discipline your son, you reveal that you want him to die without hope — and that betrays a terrible lack of love.

The best and most effective kind of discipline always comes bundled with large doses of love. That is why two key verses directed especially to fathers warn against applying discipline in an unloving way.

"Fathers, do not exasperate your children," says Paul in Ephesians 6:4 (NIV). What does he mean? According to one Bible scholar, "The gospel introduced a fresh element into parental responsibility by insisting that the feelings of the child must be taken into consideration. In a society where the father's authority was absolute, this was revolutionary. . . . Above all else, he warns them against goading their children into a state of perpetual resentment (cf. 4:26). He is not thinking of extreme instances like disinheritance, but the everyday tensions of family life. Fathers must not make unreasonable demands. Otherwise

children, being overcor-
rected, may lose heart.
Children should be treated
with tenderness."[2]

In other words, make
sure that you discipline
your kids with love.

In Colossians 3:21,
Paul takes a slightly different tack. "Fathers," he
writes, "do not embitter
your children, or they will
become discouraged." This
means that dads "must not
challenge their children's
resistance by an unreasonable exercise of authority.
Firm discipline may be
necessary, but it must always be administered in the
right spirit. Parents should
not give in to fault-find-
ing, nor always be nagging
their children. The reason
for this counsel is that 'they
will become discouraged.'

Checking the facts

78% Parental influence

40% Sibling Influence

40% of teens in the United States indicate that their brothers and sisters have a lot of influence in their life.

78% of American teens say that their parents have a lot of influence on their life.

(1997) www.barna.org

Parents can be so exacting, so demanding, or so severe that they create within their children the feeling that it is impossible for them to please. The Greek word used here has in it the idea of 'losing heart' and suggests going about in a listless or sullen attitude."[3]

Again, discipline your children with love. Always with love!

Remedial Discipline

One big part of biblical discipline is correction. When our children step outside of a boundary we have clearly set, they need to be corrected. We need to put them back on a healthy and constructive path.

Correction is an act of love. If you don't believe in correcting your children, you don't believe that God corrects you. And if God doesn't correct you, Scripture says you are not a son or a daughter of God (see Heb. 12:5–11). The very nature of loving involves correction.

Let me name just one example here. It amazes me how some parents allow their children to make fun of other kids. We should never tolerate such a thing. Our kids may do this behind our back, but if we find out about it, we need to correct them, firmly and in love. Depending upon the age of the child, sometimes that may involve physical consequences, like spanking.

"Do you mean to tell me that you believe in the physical abuse of children?" you ask. No, I don't; but I do believe in biblical discipline. And at times that may involve "the rod."

A child who grows up making fun of other children is making fun of God's creation, and that never pleases God. God not only wants us to love Him, He wants us to love others in the same way we want to be loved. As parents, we must train our children in this habit. And when we need to correct them, we need to step up to the plate.

Some of us struggle with this because we have

Correction is an act of love.

a flawed goal in life: we want to be popular with our kids. But God did not call you and me to be popular with our kids; God calls us to parent our children according to His Word. And that Word calls for us to exercise loving correction whenever necessary. We ought to love our kids enough to discipline them fairly and firmly, regardless of the consequences to our current popularity around the house.

Positive Discipline

Correction is only part of biblical discipline. If our main goal is to educate our kids so that they eagerly walk with God, then a large portion of our discipline should focus on "preventive measures." And the sooner we do this, the less correction we will generally have to administer.

Why do most kids go astray? One big reason is peer pressure; that's why we need to get involved in our children's choices of friends. But even when they have great friends, they can

> *We need to teach our children how to stand alone.*

find themselves in situations where peer pressure urges

them and needles them into doing what they know to be wrong. Here's where a positive aspect of discipline can be so helpful. We need to teach our children how to stand alone.

I will never forget something that Chuck Swindoll said some time ago: "The greatest thing you can teach your child is how to stand alone." That takes discipline. If your child understands from an early age that it's not about what everybody else wants or what everybody else needs, but about what God wants, he or she has a better chance of standing alone when the time comes. Teach your child how to stand alone — and if that means lonely times on Friday night, then so be it. If that means your kid's the only one, then so be it. If they don't learn how to stand alone, then they are likely to end up in a big-time mess when they get on their own. Teach them *now* how to stand alone!

Second, teach them the discipline of memorizing Scripture. Children need to learn the value of memorizing Bible verses. I remember my mother sitting me down and teaching me to memorize Scripture. I remember going to vacation Bible school as a little boy, learning to memorize passages from God's Word. From a very young age, the Word of God needs to be tucked securely in the heart of your child. If you have preschoolers, don't assume they have to be nine before they understand. Don't wait! Teach them the Word of God, help them to memorize the Word of God, put the Word of God in their heart so that they will not sin against God.

Even to this day, I often find myself in situations where some of those Bible passages that my mother taught me so long ago come back to mind, helping me to avoid making a wrong choice. I taught my own children to memorize Scripture. Sometimes they liked it, sometimes they didn't. None of that mattered. What matters is that the Word of God needs to be implanted in the heart of our children. And the sooner, the better.

The Result of Biblical Discipline

I have a friend who may owe his success in life to an unstolen Styrofoam ball.

My friend's almost 50, but this part of his story goes all the way back to a warm spring day in grade school. Around noon that day he and a dozen or so friends made their way to a fast food restaurant a couple of blocks from school. When the noisy group reached the parking lot, the most "popular" boy saw some bright green Styrofoam balls waving from the top of several

car antennas. He thought it would be fun to steal them, and the others quickly agreed. Quickly they fanned out across the parking lot, happily snatching the ugly promotional gimmicks from the unoccupied cars.

All except for my friend. He stood there, frozen.

While the others called to him to join their petty larceny, he remembered his parents' Christian instruction. While his friends filled their pockets with useless plastic balls, he remembered several Bible verses he had memorized. And in a few moments, disregarding his friends' catcalls, he slowly turned around and headed back to school, alone.

On a universal scale of important events, that one doesn't seem to rank very high, does it? Or . . . does it? My friend traces his ability to stand alone for his Lord — something he's had to do several times since then, in much more important ways — back to that warm spring day in the restaurant parking lot when, as a fifth grader, he decided to do what he thought was right, regardless.

That's the value of biblical discipline, parents. It may cost a little, but it pays big dividends in the end. And those dividends just keep on paying, year after year.

> *. . . the Word of God needs to be implanted in the heart of our children.*

Endnotes

1 R. Laird Harris, Gleason L. Archer, and Bruce K. Walke, "Yasar" in *Theological Wordbook of the Old Testament*, Vol. 1 (Chicago, IL: Moody Press, 1980), p. 387.

2 A. Skevington Wood, "Ephesians" in Frank E Gaebelein, general editor, *The Expositor's Bible Commentary*, Vol. 11 (Grand Rapids, MI: Zondervan Publishing House, 1978), p. 81–82.

3 Curtis Vaughan, "Colossians" in Frank E. Gaebelein, general editor, *The Expositor's Bible Commentary*, Vol. 11 (Grand Rapids, MI: Zondervan Publishing House, 1978), p. 219.

Chapter 5

Eliminate All Unnecessary Stuff

IN just three short seasons, "American Idol" has become a television phenomenon. Millions tune in each week to see whether their favorites will get the nod from viewers to continue their quest for stardom.

In season number one, Kelly Clarkson, a 20-year-old from Burleson, Texas, won it all. When Kelly released her first album, it instantly rose to number one on the *Billboard* charts. In season number two, Ruben Studdard followed her, and in season number three, Fantasia Barrino added her name to the growing list of American idols.

As popular as all three young people have become, however, I believe they all

What is the Number One American idol today, even among Christians? Don't let this shock you, but it's the family. As author Robert McQuilkin states in a book called *An Introduction to Biblical Ethics*, "A new idolatry has crept into evangelical thinking: the idolatry of family."

The Bible teaches that an idol is anything or anyone that we place before God. The Scripture forbids us to put anything or anyone before our God — and yet, in many of our homes, the family has usurped God's rightful place. We have allowed soccer, football, basketball, cheerleading, drill team, band, and a host of other "good"

lag way behind America's true Number One idol. Can you guess what it is? Jesus Christ alludes to it in Luke 14:26.

If anyone comes to Me and does not hate his father and mother, and children, brothers, and sisters, yes, and his own life also, he cannot be My disciple.

activities to take priority in our children's lives. We've even encouraged it. Yet Jesus tells us that the priority for you and your kids ought to be *God*. That means there's only one thing to do: eliminate all unnecessary stuff.

The Birth of a Little God

Today a large number of professing Christians demonstrate an appalling lack of commitment to Christ, all in the name of the family. We have taken our families and made them into little gods, placing them before God, His church, and His kingdom.

I wonder what Jesus would say about that?

Many of us go from weekend to weekend, never thinking about how God fits into our busy schedules. We literally follow our children around the countryside, allowing their agendas to run our lives. We run from game to tournament to exhibition to competition, all in the name of family — and all the while neglecting the rightful place of God and His church and kingdom. For

You have to love Me more than anyone and anything else in life.

too many of us, the family has become a little god.

Jesus says that we must be willing to *hate* our father and mother, wife and children, brothers and sisters, and even our own life, for His sake. What does He mean? Surely he doesn't suggest that we should despise these people? What is he saying?

Jesus means that we have to love Him far more than we love any of these others. If He were here today, I believe He'd say to us, "You are out of balance! You have to love Me more than anyone and anything else in life. This is the key to a successful family life." If we neglect His instruction, very quickly we become the midwife at the birth of a little god. Our children become

our idol. Our marriage becomes our idol.

And God gets shunted off to one side.

The Death of a Little God

Jesus has no interest in allowing us to divide our loyalties. He wants us to kill and destroy all gods who clamor for the place that belongs to Him alone. Therefore, He calls all Christians to three decisive actions. Listen to his call to arms in Luke 14:27–33:

> And whoever does not bear His cross and come after Me, cannot be My disciple.
> For which of you intending to build a tower, does not sit down first and count

the cost, whether he has enough to finish it? Lest after he has laid the foundation and is not able to finish, all who see it would begin to mock him, saying, "This man began to build and was not able to finish."

Or what king, going to make war against another king, does not sit down first and consider whether he is able with 10,000 to meet him who comes against him with 20,000? Or else while the other is still a great way off, he sends a delegation and asks conditions of peace. So likewise, whoever of you does not forsake all he has, cannot be my disciple.

Jesus calls all Christians to three decisive actions: *bear*, *count*, and *forsake*.

1. Bear the cross

What does it mean to bear the cross? The cross was nothing to be proud of in the first century. Back then, it was not a beautiful piece of jewelry. The cross represented the most humiliating, tragic, painful and shameful death that anyone could ever face.

Usually the Romans would strip the condemned

man and drive him naked to the place of his execution, just outside the city where everyone could watch. The authorities crucified their enemies in a prominent location as a potent reminder of the brutal authority of Rome. It was meant as a means of control and intimidation.

When Jesus told us to bear the cross, He meant that we must be willing to experience shame, humiliation, and pain for His sake. We are to publicly identify with Him, regardless of the cost. This requires us to operate by a different code and a unique set of operational procedures.

God did not put us here to do what the world suggests or demands of us. We are to live by a different set of guidelines. We must be different; we

The cross was nothing to be proud of in the first century.

must be willing to bear the cross. And if this brings us humiliation, shame, and suffering, we have to be willing to bear it. So the Bible tells us, "If you suffer, it should not be as a murderer or thief or any other kind of criminal, or even as a meddler. However, if you suffer as a Christian, do not be ashamed, but praise God that you bear that name" (1 Pet. 4:15–16; NIV).

Jesus says to us, "You must love Me more than you love your family. You must love Me more than you love your kids." Jesus calls us to sell out to Him, body and soul. He instructs us to put our family in its proper place, without allowing it to become a little god. "Bear the cross," He tells us.

Jesus reminds us that if we are going to become what He calls us to be, we must count the cost.

2. Count the cost

Jesus gives two illustrations about counting the cost, the first about building a tower and the other about planning for war. He uses both to picture the same principle: there is a high cost in following Him as Lord and Savior. Jesus reminds us that if we are going to become what He calls us to be, we must count the cost.

Of course, it costs a lot more *not* to follow Him.

Many families today have failed to count the cost of putting their child's athletic career or academic future ahead of their walk with Christ. Sports and academics are good when pursued in balance, but when we allow them to become an idol, we gravely hurt our kids. We need to teach our children something far greater and longer lasting than how to succeed at football or forensics. We need to teach them how to become an uncompromising disciple for the Lord Jesus Christ.

Parents, God has put *you* in charge of your children. As such, He will hold you accountable for the value systems you teach them. Kids can smell hypocrisy a thousand miles away. You can talk Jesus, you can preach Jesus, and you can read to them from the Bible — but if you do not model before them that God is your top priority, you are hurting rather than helping them.

Checking the facts

70%

53%

Mothers

Fathers

70% of teens have daily conversations with their mothers about an important issue in their life, compared to the 53% of teens who have a similar type of conversation with their fathers.

(1998) www.barna.org

3. Forsake all

Jesus says to us, "So likewise, whoever of you who does not forsake all that he has, cannot be my disciple" (Luke 14:33). The term translated "forsake" means to "say goodbye to it all." Are you saying goodbye to some "good" things in life in order to pursue the "best" thing of loving and serving God?

To forsake also means "to renounce." Are you renouncing those things that contradict God's way? Are you eliminating them? Jesus calls us to absolute and unconditional surrender. Don't forget His memorable exchange with the man in Luke 9. When Jesus told the fellow to follow Him, the man answered, "Lord, first let me go and bury my father." Do you remember Jesus' answer? He said, "Let the dead bury their own dead, but you go and proclaim the kingdom of God" (Luke 9:59–60).

When Jesus calls, we cannot reply, "Wait a minute! Let me check and see what is on for this weekend, whether our family has plans. If we don't have a tournament, we'll come." Jesus says that if you want to follow Him, you must be willing to forsake all.

What Kind of Salt Are You?

Why is this issue so important? Why should it have a place in a book on parenting? Jesus gives us the answer in Luke 9:34–35.

> Salt is good, but if the salt has lost its flavor, how shall it be seasoned? It is neither fit for the land, nor for the dunghill, but men throw it out. He who has ears to hear, let him hear.

If you are a believer in Christ, Jesus compares you to "salt." Do you know what salt does? Salt preserves. In this decaying society of ours, Jesus says that you and I — and our kids — are here to slow the rate of spiritual and moral decay. We are to be *different*. Salt is powerful because it is different.

It is different from the substance on which it is sprinkled. But how can salt exercise its power if it loses its flavor, its difference?

We are to be different.

There's a lot at stake here. Jesus calls us to be salt, to keep our testimony strong. If you know Christ as your Savior, then God has made you into a walking billboard for Him. Your testimony is at stake, and there is nothing more precious than your testimony. It may be kind of corny, but the old statement is really true: "You are the only

Bible that some people will read." Your testimony *matters*. So keep it full of salt.

God has called you to model before the world a proper value system. He calls you to mentor, to teach, and to train your children in proper values. And what is a value? A value is something you regard as special and important. What are you showing your kids that has special importance in your life? What is of real value to you? What are your kids picking up from you?

We tried to teach our kids the importance of family — not the unbiblical and unbalanced view so popular today, but a right and balanced perspective in relationship to the rest of life. We did family vacations. One night a week we went out to eat together. This practice changed as the boys grew older, but we adjusted and kept committed to various family matters.

Remember, your kids are going to model what you do, not what you say. They are going to become what you are, not what you are trying to project.

A Concern for the Next Generation

Jesus calls us to be different, to be salt, to model godly values. Why? Because He is very concerned about the next generation. He wants to make sure that

the next generation doesn't end up in the garbage heap — where unsavory salt goes — because its members have never been taught to bear the cross, count the cost, and forsake all.

God is calling families back into perspective, back into balance. God didn't call any of us to make our little kids rich. He didn't call any of us to make our little kids famous. Of course, if you can do that for them along the way, go for it. Enjoy! But that is never His ultimate call. That is never the most important thing. That is never the central thing. Your call, like mine, is to train up your kids in the way they should go, so that when they are old, they will not depart from it (see Prov. 22:6). Your call, like mine, is to train them up to love the Lord their God with all their heart, with all of their soul, and with all of their strength.

Do you love the Lord more than you love this world? Do you love Him more than you love your kids, more than you love your grandchildren? Do you love Him more than you love anything else? That is the call of Jesus.

In the House of Dagon

Long ago in battle the Philistines captured the ark of God from the Israelites (see 1 Sam. 5:1–5). They took it to the temple of Dagon, their pagan god. They placed the ark beside the idol of Dagon, to picture Dagon's superiority to the God of the Hebrews. And then they went to bed.

The next morning, when the Philistines awoke and returned to the house of Dagon, they found their idol on its face before the ark of God — strange, but fixable. So they propped their little god back up and went about their business.

The next day when they returned once more, they found Dagon again fallen on his face before the ark of God — but this time, his head and hands had been broken off. They saw Dagon lying helpless at the foot of the ark of the covenant . . . a powerful reminder that every "god" will bow to the King of kings and the Lord of lords.

We should not think that our story will be any different from theirs. Every little god whom we foolishly worship *will* one day bow to the King of kings and the Lord of lords. Dagon represents all of the little gods that we serve, including kids and family. If we try to set them before the God of heaven, God will do to our little gods the same as He did to Dagon. He will judge them. He will not allow any other gods before Him. God never has and never will permit His people to put anything or anyone above Him.

It's not about our families and about our kids all the time. It's all about Jesus. It's all about Christ and following Him. That is the commitment that God expects us to make, above everything else.

Parents, eliminate all unnecessary stuff in your life; then do the same thing in the lives of your kids. Remember Dagon, fallen on his face before the Lord, his head and hands broken off. Eliminate all unnecessary stuff . . . before the King of heaven decides to do it for you.

> . . . *eliminate all unnecessary stuff in your life; then do the same thing in the lives of your kids.*

Chapter 6

Love Them Unconditionally

SHORTLY after he became a father for the first time, author Floyd McClung visited the home of a good friend. This man had an eight-month-old daughter whom he was preparing to put to bed. As he happily cuddled her, he kept repeating some words that Floyd had never expected to hear.

"You're mine," he said softly. "I want you. Nobody can take you away from me. You belong to me. I love you!"

Those simple words had a profound effect on Floyd. "I had never heard a father speak like this to his child," he admitted. Those few precious moments taught Floyd that "warmth is an essential characteristic for a husband and a father.

It is a manly, masculine trait that gives tremendous strength to his family and provides a massive support framework for everyone in his home. By his warmth, a father says to his wife and children, 'I like you. In fact, I find you irresistible.' "[1]

Whether you are a father or a mother, God calls you to love your children unconditionally, from the time they're born. Let them often hear words like the following from your lips: "I want you to know that whatever you do, whatever you say, I'm going to love you without fail and without condition." Keep putting that thought in their little minds when they're young. And do it consistently, continually, perpetually.

But What About . . . ?

When I speak like this to many parents, they have a simple response. "Pastor," they say, "if you only knew what my kid was involved in! He's driving me crazy."

Kids driving parents crazy, of course, is part and parcel of parenting. But let me ask you something:

do you think *your* conduct ever tests God? Do you think you always act in a way that He considers respectful, wise, honorable? If you answer, "Yes," then you're either insensitive or a liar. All of us mess up in more ways than we can count.

But what does God do? He continues to love us unconditionally. He loves us the way we are. He wants us to change and gives us

> . . . *unconditional love has a power that blows everything else away.*

the resources to become more like His Son, of course, but He never tells us, "If you do this and that, then I suppose I might love you." No! He loves you just the way you are.

God models for us the way we are to love our own children. It isn't always easy and it doesn't always feel rewarding. But unconditional love has a power that blows everything else away.

In his excellent devotional book, *Moments for Families with Prodigals*, author and pastor Robert J. Morgan recounts many of his own struggles with offspring who, at least for a time, rejected their Christian heritage. He writes:

Some time ago while feeling in low spirits over a struggling child, I spoke with a woman in Philadelphia who attended a seminar I was conducting. She seemed radiant and cheerful, but her smile faded as she told me of her own son, far from the Lord, who had broken her heart. "I prayed for him a long time," she said, "then I sort of ran out of prayers."

At the same seminar another woman told me of a daughter who had become deeply ensnared in demonism, witchcraft, and the occult.

"When she came back to the Lord," said the woman, "she credited my prayers and those of my friends. 'I didn't have a chance against your prayers, Mom,' she told me."

Morgan concludes, "Prodigals have a way of coming home."[2]

Indeed they do. But before that day, when they're in the middle of some sin — and all of our children will periodically get into some degree of sin, because they're sinners, just like their parents — you can say to them, "Remember what I've been telling you since you were a little child? I just wanted you to know that although I do not agree with what you're doing, I still love you unconditionally. It doesn't matter what you do or what you say or how your choices hurt us. I want you to know this: when you lay your head on the pillow every night of your life, Mom and Dad love you unconditionally."

No wonder the Scripture tells us, "Love covers over a multitude of sins" (1 Pet. 4:8; NIV).

Love Them With Words

Mom and Dad, build up your child with loving words. Your children will believe what you say to them.

I tried to make this a regular practice with my boys. I would often say to them, "I want you to know that I believe in you. No one believes in you more than your dad," or, "I am your biggest fan, and don't you ever forget it."

Kids need to know that their fathers and mothers believe in them. Periodically, write a little note or letter to your son or daughter and conclude it, "I want you to know that I believe in you." Your children need to know that *someone* believes in them.

Are you letting your kids know that you believe in them?

Do everything you can with your words to build

up your children. Discouraging and hurtful words can cause a great deal of damage. Many years ago a teacher told me that I was stupid. Her stinging words drove me to extreme efforts in order to prove her wrong, to prove to myself that I really was not stupid. When I got my ACT scores back, of course, it became very obvious to everyone that she had been somewhat correct. But you know what? Today I hold a doctoral degree and she doesn't.

Speak good words to your children. Even when you have to correct them, speak to them in a positive way. Let them know of your constant love. Don't train them to cringe every time you open your mouth; instead, train them to expect blessing rather than curses. Love them unconditionally with your words.

Are you letting your kids know that you believe in them?

Love Them with Action

Love is not merely a matter of words; real love also takes action. It gets busy. It works to express itself. So love your children with your actions.

Here's one activity you might not have thought about: how about praying and fasting for your kids? That has to be one of the most tangible ways you can show them your love. I'll never forget the day James Dobson of Focus on the Family told me, "You know, Shirley and I have fasted and prayed for our kids for many years. One week, I will pray and fast for the kids; the next week, she will pray and fast for the kids, one day a week."

Early in my parenting years I made a com-

> *. . . don't dump your complaints and disappointments about the church in front of your kids.*

mitment to pray and fast for my boys. I still do it, although both of them are out of the house.

Have you ever prayed and fasted for the spiritual vitality and success of your kids? It's one significant way you can demonstrate your unconditional love for them.

Here's a second practical way to show your unconditional love for your children: get your kids actively connected to a local church. Help them to get involved in its various ministries.

If as a parent you convey cynicism about the church, you are going to raise kids who are deeply cynical about the church — and don't forget, Christ died for that church. You demonstrate unconditional love for your children when you show them your love for your church, your love for your pastor, your love for your other ministers. Whatever you do, don't dump your complaints and disappointments about the church in front of your kids. If you need to dump, then back up your truck and dump your load in a pastor's office. The worst thing you can do is to create negativity about the church in your family. If you do that now, you'll reap a horrible whirlwind later. You'll create nothing but bitterness, suspicion, and cynicism in the hearts of your kids — and that hardly reflects unconditional love.

We did our best to teach our boys the importance of church. We mentored them in the importance of church. We taught them to love all of the church's ministers and all the of the church's ministries. When people asked me how to pray for my kids, I always told them two things:

1. Pray that my kids will grow up loving Jesus;

2. Pray that my kids will grow up loving the church.

So many preachers' kids struggle with both of these things. But I thank God that our gracious God answered the prayers of so many! Today, our kids love the Lord and the church for which He died.

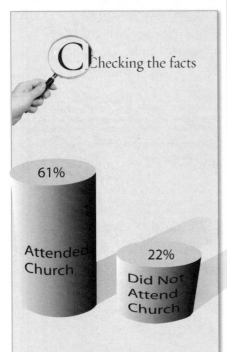

Checking the facts

61%

Attended Church

22%

Did Not Attend Church

Adults who attended church regularly as a child are nearly three times as likely to be attending a church today as are their peers who avoided the church during childhood (61% to 22%, respectively). www.barna.org

And you know what else? They know, by our actions, that we love them unconditionally. Whatever may happen in the future, we'll continue to love them. We see that not only as our solemn duty before God, but as our great privilege. And you want to know something else? It works.

Several years ago a heartwarming letter appeared in the Ann Landers advice column. One reader wrote:

I have read so many letters in your column from people who have no respect, let alone love, for their relatives. This one will be different.

When my mother died three years ago, she left a small amount of disability insurance that was divided in equal amounts among her six children. Since our eldest sister had taken care of Dad for eight years and then cared for Mom until she passed away, I felt that she should have my share of the money.

You can imagine how happy I was when I arrived at my sister's home and found that my brother had already sent her his check. He had decided quietly on his own, as I did, that our sister who took care of Dad and Mom should have his share of the inheritance.

> *They know, by our actions, that we love them unconditionally.*

Mom left no big estate. There was just the old house where we were all born and the little property it sat on. The property, with every family member's consent, was sold immediately after the funeral. The proceeds were divided between that wonderful eldest sister and another sister who had never married. Our unmarried sister had lived in apartments most of her life, and we decided that she should have a little home of her own. We all had dinner together one night and my brother greeted Sis like this:

"Well, they're breaking the ground for construction on

Children learn to act in a loving way from parents who demonstrate unconditional love.

your home. It will be down the block from us."

"Home? What home?" she asked.

"YOUR home, Sis. Congratulations!"

There was a lot of whooping and hollering and a few tears. It was a thrill for us just to see the look on her face.

Last week I received a check in the mail from my unmarried sister. It was my share of Mom's government bonds. I called Sis and told her I was returning the check to her. She said, "You can't do that. My feelings will be hurt." Can you imagine? She insisted that I take the money, buy something lovely for my daughters, and tell them it was from their grandmother, purchased with the last bit of money she had left behind for us.

Ann, we are not wealthy people. We are all underpaid Texas teachers who have always lived from paycheck to paycheck, but I consider myself very lucky to have been born into a family that is so loving and generous.

I know this letter is too darned long to publish, but I did have a lot of fun writing it.

Ann wrote back, "What a terrific upper. After reading thousands of letters from family members who are at war over money, it's a privilege to print a letter like yours. Too bad your parents didn't leave behind a book on how to raise children."[3]

Children learn to act in a loving way from parents who demonstrate unconditional love. These Texas parents may not have written a book like the one you're holding, but they did leave behind a book in the lives of their children.

And that's nothing but a great read featuring the unmistakable footprints of unconditional love.

Love Them Regardless

Regardless of what your kids are doing, love them unconditionally. Regardless of the lifestyle they have adopted, love them unconditionally. Regardless of what they're up to, love them unconditionally.

You can love them and still hate what they are involved in. You can love them and despise the sin that has trapped them. But if they have strayed, you will never win them back through any way other than unconditional love.

Robert Morgan knows about both the struggle of a child who wanders spiritually and the power of unconditional love. I'd like to end this chapter with some thoughts and a prayer of his.

One Saturday night, on the last day of March, as I tried to ward off worry long enough to prepare the next day's sermon, the following words came to mind as a prayer for my child. I jotted them in the flyleaf of my Bible and have been offering them as a prayer ever since.

Lord,
Remember

_____

Reclaim him from Satan.

Restrain him from evil.

Rebuke errant patterns in his life.

Rectify any careless ways.

Rekindle his spiritual fervor and revive his soul.

Reassure him of Your plan for him.

Reinforce his faith.

Release Your Spirit into his heart and Recruit him for Your kingdom's work. In Jesus' name. Amen.

Endnotes

1 Floyd McClung, *God's Man in the Family* (Eugene, OR: Harvest House, 1994), p. 83.

2 Robert J. Morgan, *Moments for Families with Prodigals* (Colorado Springs, CO: NavPress, 2003), p. 17.

3 Ann Landers, "Parents Left Behind a Legacy of Love," *Dallas Morning News*, March 21, 1991, p. 2C.

Our tendency is to grab and hold our children and not allow them to make mistakes. Then, when they do fail, we jump forward to bail them out and prevent them from learning valuable lessons.

– James Dobson

The Only Perfect Parent

WHAT is a parent? A parent is a mentor, a teacher, and a coach.

A mentor models right.

A teacher teaches right.

A coach shows how to do right.

After saying all of that, however, I think it's important to remember that the only perfect parent is God — and yet He has more kids out of fellowship with Him than any of us have! In an odd sort of way, I think that thought can give us encouragement and comfort in our role as parents.

Samson, Revisited

Maybe you have children who have turned away from God. Perhaps your children have gotten involved in things that break

Manoah asked God for wisdom on how to raise his son in a godly home. Samson had faithful parents and God greatly used Samson. This strong man began his life with God — but he ended it in disobedience, far from the righteous example of his parents.

Don't ever forget that *a godly home is no guarantee of a godly life*. A child can reject the spiritual influence of his or her parents. Remember, God is a perfect parent. He never made a parenting mistake. He is the perfect Father. Yet He has countless wayward children.

your heart. Maybe they have caused you untold disappointment, pain, and heartache.

If your kids are in that place of rebellion, please hear me: it doesn't mean it's your fault! Stop letting Satan beat up on you over your children.

Remember Manoah and his son, Samson, whom we met in chapter one?

If you talk to 50 parents, all with grown children who love and serve the Lord in a local church, and you ask them, "How did your kids turn out like that?" they all have the same answer. Every time I've asked this question of somebody who appeared to have successful kids, they've told me the same thing: "Chalk it up to the grace of God." Certainly they have applied some biblical principles that served as effective conduits of grace, but the ultimate answer comes down to the grace of God.

Maybe you did everything right, and yet your children still went their own way. It might be happening right now. If that describes you, don't give up. You still have a job to do.

Get back on your knees before God and pray that the Lord will draw your kids back to himself. Pray that He will pour out His grace on their lives, despite their disobedience. And pray that soon you will be able to rejoice with them in their wholehearted return to the Savior.

And if that doesn't describe you, get on your knees and thank God. It's only by His grace that you are where you are.

Let us not fool ourselves — without Christianity, without Christian education, without the principles of Christ inculcated into young life, we are simply rearing pagans. – *Peter Marshall*

A Time for Joy

For many years I never preached on the topic of parenting. I had two reasons. First, I didn't want to put my kids on display. And second, I didn't know how it was all going to turn out.

Today one of my sons is a student at Liberty University, planning on going into the pastoral ministry. Another son is married and works as the offensive coordinator for the football team at a large high school in the Little Rock area.

I have a pretty good idea how they're both going to turn out.

As I look back over almost a quarter century of parenting, I ask myself, "What did we really teach our children?" We mentored, taught, and coached them to love Jesus, to love their family, to love their church. Praise God, they got it! And thank God, I believe they got it in that order.

I love it when I hear Nick stand up and proclaim the Word of God.

That has brought me a great thrill. I love it on Friday nights when I watch my other son call plays. That is awesome. (I told him he needs to give me a headset and the team would be a lot better. But he said, "Dad, I want to give you a headset, but you will not be able to speak to me or hear me." And what fun is there in that?)

But would you like to know the most reward-ing thing of all for me as a parent? It's when one of my sons says to me, "Dad, our pastor knocked it over the fence today. We're growing like crazy; in fact, they're talking about going to another service. This is *great!*" That excites me. Or when one of them calls me on Saturday and says, "Dad, I'm praying for you tomorrow." That, my friend, brings unbelievable comfort and strength to the heart of this parent. So let me urge you one last time:

Mentor your kids!
Teach your kids!
Coach your kids!

And then plead for the grace of God to make the following verse a reality in your life:

The father of a righ-teous man has great joy; he who has a wise son delights in him (Prov. 23:24; NIV).

In January 1992, at one a.m., one very tired mom heard a cough. I bolted from my sleep to a standing/running position and in one leap made it to the bathroom and flipped on the light to find my six-year-old daughter sitting on the edge of the tub. The stuff from her tummy was all over the floor, the lid of the toilet, and herself. I proceeded to clean the floor and surrounding areas, then placed Sarah into the tub to wash down. As I turned on the shower, Sarah said, "Mom," with a wrinkled nose and a hesitant voice, "I threw up on Collett too."

Collett is her nine-year-old sister, who happens to share the bed. I closed the curtain and ran to see. I met Collett in the hallway, and she said Sarah had thrown up on her. I turned on the bedroom light and much to my amazement, there was the dreaded sight of Sarah's dinner on five blankets, two pillows, two sheets, a baby blanket, and Collett's pajamas. I bundled it all up into the bottom sheet and placed it at the back door. I put fresh bedding on the bed and placed a bucket beside Sarah, then I crawled back in my own bed. At which time, my well-covered, half-asleep husband inquired, "What's wrong?"

— *Focus on the Family Newsletter*

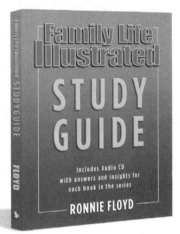

Also by Dr. Ronnie Floyd . . .

5 1/4 x 8 3/8 • Paper • 128 pages
• *INCLUDES AUDIO CD*
ISBN 0-89221-599-2

Special Features Include:

• Study questions in each book for reflection and to aid
  small-group study

• Study guide that works for all six books that also includes
  an audio CD from Dr. Floyd with answers and insights for
  each book.

Available at Christian bookstores nationwide.

ISBN 0-89221-586-0

It seems like everything keeps changing and no one understands. Every day seems to bring more pivotal decisions to be made. Life is complicated and stressful, and you feel you are alone! Fight the isolation – don't be a spectator in your own life! Get powerful solutions and strategies to survive and thrive during the toughest time of your life – and find out how to rely on God when life overwhelms you!

Money, debt, credit card complications — believe it or not, the Bible can be the most practical guide to financial management you will ever find! Simple, easy-to-implement solutions don't require high cost solutions or painful personal concessions. Don't do without the answers which can help change your financial future and solve a critical area of stress affecting you, your family, or even your marriage. Invest in God's wisdom, and reap the blessings He has in store for you!

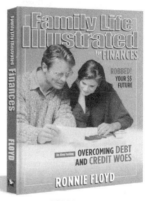

ISBN 0-89221-587-9

ISBN 0-89221-584-4

Your job, your finances, your friends – nothing you ever do will matter as much as being a good parent to your child. Going beyond the surface strategies and quick psychobabble solutions, this book reveals solid, God-based insight on becoming a more effective parent. Don't choose to struggle alone — tap into the wealth of wisdom God wants to share with you and find how you can make a positive, remarkable, and lasting change in the lives of your children today!

Also by Dr. Ronnie Floyd . . .

Thought about your marriage lately? Or do you just take it for granted? Marriage is not a passive enterprise – it takes skill, work, and attention if you want it to survive in the "disposable" culture of our society today. Do you have the marriage God wants you to have? Tired of going through the motions, feeling helpless to make the change for the better you know you need to make? It's time to take control and make your marriage be the true partnership that God designed. Don't wait to make a renewed commitment for marital success!

ISBN 0-89221-585-2

ISBN 0-89221-583-6

Are you happening to life or is life simply happening to you? Overwhelmed, overworked, stressed, and tired, it's easy to lose sight of things important to you as a woman, wife, and perhaps even a mother. Be empowered, be decisive, and be open to God's gently guiding hand in your life! God can be what you need – He can strengthen, calm, and sustain you when life seems impossible. No matter what you face, God can give you the knowledge and wisdom to adapt, endure, and affect a change!

The Gay Agenda is a compelling and compassionate look at one of the most turbulent issues of our society today – homosexuality and same-sex marriage. Dr. Ronnie Floyd states the importance of maintaining the traditional family, while revealing the homosexual agenda at work in our schools, churches, and government. He also looks at the ongoing controversies over gay clergy, and turns the spotlight on judicial activism as well. Dr. Floyd makes clear the political chaos and confusion of this election-year hot potato as both major parties seek to find political payoffs on these issues. *The Gay Agenda* cannot be ignored.

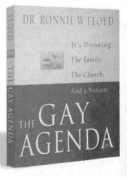

ISBN: 0-89221-582-8

Available at Christian bookstores nationwide.

Recognizing the vital importance of the family in the success of not only individuals, but for our society today, the "Family Life Illustrated" series offers real answers for real-life problems being faced each day by families. Articulate, informative, and always relevant — Dr. Ronnie Floyd is reaching the hearts of millions weekly through his broadcast ministry Invitation to Life, aired on WGN's Superstation and other television networks nationally each week. An accomplished author of 17 books as well as a powerful group speaker, Dr. Floyd has over 27 years of ministry experience and is senior pastor for a congregation of 15,000 in Northwest Arkansas. Dr. Floyd has been been seen on Fox News, WorldNetDaily, Janet Parshall's America, Washington Watch, USA Radio Network, FamilyNet, and more!

MORE RESOURCES FROM
DR. RONNIE W. FLOYD

CD/VHS/DVD
"Family Life Illustrated Series"

CD/VHS/DVD
"The Gay Agenda"

Other Books By Dr. Floyd
Life on Fire
How to Pray
The Power of Prayer and Fasting
The Meaning of a Man

Weekly International Television and Internet

Sundays: (7:30 a.m. CST) WGN SUPERSTATION

Thursdays: (9:00 p.m. CST) Daystar Christian Television Network

Sundays: (9:15 a.m. CST) Live webcast on
www.fbcspringdale.org

For more information on all resources: www.invitationtolife.org

For information about our church:
www.fbcspringdale.org   www.churchph.com

or call (479) 751-4523 and ask for Invitation to Life